she
followed
the
moon
back to
herself

amanda lovelace

Andrews McMeel
PUBLISHING®

also by amanda lovelace

the
women are some kind of magic
poetry series:

the princess saves herself in this one (#1)
the witch doesn't burn in this one (#2)
the mermaid's voice returns in this one (#3)

slay those dragons: a journal for writing your own story

believe in your own magic: a 45-card oracle deck & guidebook

***

the
things that h(a)unt
poetry duology:

to make monsters out of girls (#1)
to drink coffee with a ghost (#2)

***

the
you are your own fairy tale
poetry trilogy:

break your glass slippers (#1)
shine your icy crown (#2)
unlock your storybook heart (#3)

***

flower crowns & fearsome things
(a standalone poetry collection)

she
followed
the
moon
back to
herself

amanda lovelace

cozy witch tarot: a 78-card tarot deck & guidebook

cozy witch tarot coloring book

***

*make your own magic: a beginner's guide to
self-empowering witchcraft*

*your magical journal: a place for self-reflection,
spellwork, & making your own magic*

*your magical life: a young witch's guide
to becoming happy, confident, & powerful*

to the woman going through
the darkest night of her soul—

don't give up yet.

it gets better.
it always gets better.

trigger warning

this book contains
sensitive material relating to:

body image issues,
eating disorders,
self-injury,
alcoholism,
misogyny,
religion,
suicide,
death,
trauma,

& possibly more.

remember to practice self-care
before, during, & after
reading.

a note from the author

dear reader,

i began my writing career by publishing extremely personal poetry collections that felt like happening upon a stranger's diary; especially my debut, *the princess saves herself in this one* (2017), which was the story of my life up until that point.

a few collections in, i started to feel myself getting burnt out.

i realized that i needed more time to live, to grow, & to gain some much-needed perspective before i continued writing about myself. i decided it was time to take a good, long break from that sort of poetry writing if i ever wanted to go back to it.

for that reason, the last few poetry collections i've published have been largely fictional—filled with characters of my own creation, expressing emotions & living stories similar to my own . . . but still very much fictional at their heart.

after i was done writing my last collection, *unlock your storybook heart* (2022), i'll admit that i did seriously consider walking away from poetry entirely. though those fictional collections had been an amazing exercise for my creativity, i felt like i had written about everything i've ever wanted to write about. i still didn't feel ready to write another personal collection either.

might as well end on a high note, right?

then, of course, one night, i had an idea.

the idea.

with this poetry collection, the *she* (& *they*) i write about is very much *me* again.

most (but not all) of the poems you're about to read were written during april 2023—aka national poetry month, which is a time when many poets try to write a poem a day.

i myself had only ever participated in this once before. it definitely wasn't my intention to do so that year, but the timing worked out perfectly with the conception of this collection, so i asked myself, "why the hell not?" i felt so inspired most days that i ended up writing *more* than one poem.

i guess you could say that the stars aligned.

& where there are stars, there is also the moon . . .

laced with love,
amanda

somewhere along the way
to finding herself,
she dropped her compass.

(she thinks it must have
gotten buried in the snow
somewhere.)

first, she looked to the trees,
but each & every branch
seemed so unfamiliar to her.

finally, she tipped her head back
& looked to the moon, who
drew her up to the sky & said,

"don't worry, just follow me.
try to keep in mind that
she may not be the same
as you left her, but she'll be
exactly who you need."

—*she followed the moon back to herself.*

it was under a waxing moon
that the woman had been born—

forever growing.
forever working on herself.
forever striving to be something more.

—*celestial is she.*

she was messier than
she had ever intended to be—

gossiped too much,
assumed the worst,
& put all her trust in
all the wrong people.

but

she did so many
remarkable things as well—

said the right words,
trusted her gut feelings,
& discovered who
would always be true.

—*that's just how it goes sometimes.*

her
whole
life
had to
c r u m b
           l
at her feet   *e*
before
she finally
understood
what was truly
important
to her all long.

   —her own little tower moment.

she thought she had finally found where she belonged.

it turned out she was dead wrong.

her first mistake?

thinking she could magic up a home made out of other people.

—*she's been her own sanctuary all along.*

she lost people she thought
would be part of her life forever.

she endured the sleepless nights.

she typed up dozens of texts
she could never actually
bring herself to send.

she cried so much
she thought she would
drown in a self-made sea.

they still didn't come back.

she couldn't see that,
in time, she would be fine.

—now, if anything, she thanks them for the lessons.

lately,

she's been keeping to herself.

lately,

she's been making moves in silence.

lately,

she's been putting her own healing first.

—*it's about damn time too.*

no longer does she reach for the bottle of rosé when she doesn't want to deal with the state of her life.

she makes herself confront every last bit of it—not just the joyful & floating-on-cloud-nine moments, though. she makes herself face the ugly stuff too: the unfairness, the anger, the jealousy, the resentment, & the unavoidable pain.

she's never felt more alive.

—one year sober.

she doesn't wake up hungover,
regretting the day before it even begins.

she wakes up & lets out a sigh,
relieved that she even *gets* another day.

—*birdsong alarm.*

not only is she convinced that she's right in most situations, but she's been known to cut people off without a second thought—if they wrong her, they're *gone*. just like that. she often holds a grudge for so long that she eventually forgets why she was so angry with them in the first place.

yeah, she can be a little bit of a problem sometimes.

she knows that.

—it's just that she's a scorpio.

she's intense.

she's dramatic
about everything.

she overshares,
& yet most people in her life
feel like they don't truly know her.

she's not for everyone,
& she strangely likes that.

—*it's just that she's a scorpio ii.*

when it feels like everything is spiraling out of her control, she doesn't break down.

she calmly places it in the universe's hands, fully trusting that it will take care of it.

in her experience, it always has.

when things don't work out in her favor, it's usually some sort of blessing in disguise. she knows that the universe has something else in store for her, & it will be even better, shine even brighter than she ever could have imagined.

—*she's finally woken up.*

she's done with people who
thrive off of negativity & toxicity.

she's done with people who
refuse to see their own harmful patterns.

she's done with people who
resist their own butterfly transformations.

—*she just wants some peace & quiet.*

you might not be able to tell
just by looking at her,

but she's survived things
that would defeat most.

(believe me, she knows
exactly how bad it can get.)

if you're questioning
how she laughs so freely,

then know that you're
in the presence of a woman

who refuses
to let the past win.

—*ever.*

i. she didn't deserve
   any of the suffering she went through.

ii. she wouldn't have flourished into
    the hurricane lily she is now if she hadn't.

—*maturity is realizing two truths can exist at once.*

she sleeps
better than ever

knowing that

she made
the right decisions

based on

what was
right for her at the time.

—*she can't change them, & she's stopped wanting to.*

like a moth,

she makes it her mission
to find the light in everything,

no matter how short
her life may be.

—*luna.*

at a moment's notice,

she's dancing
around her living room.

she's singing
in the passenger seat.

she can't help it—

she finally feels
safe enough to be happy.

she didn't used to
think that was possible.

—*no one is allowed to make her feel unsafe again.*

she doesn't feel the need
to count every calorie
she puts into her mouth,

        let alone
        every calorie she burns.

instead, she counts
the number of times
she sees 111, 222, & 333

on license plates,
on the clock, & while
she's scrolling on her phone—

all the proof she needs
to know that everything
is going to be alright.

—*angel numbers.*

no more contouring—
she's embracing her double chin.

no more baggy clothes—
she's embracing her big, soft belly.

no more hiding from the camera—
she's embracing her every look.

no more avoiding the people who
knew the thin version of her—
she's showing off *this* version of herself.

—in her self-acceptance era.

believe it or not,

she's well aware that
she's gained weight.

so. the. fuck. what?

she has always loved the moon
in all of her round glory,

& she has decided that

she's going to love
herself for that exact reason.

—round & glorious is she.

for the first time in years,
she wears a sleeveless shirt.

it feels almost holy to finally
allow the wind to soothe her scars.

as expected,
people stare & stare;

for the first time,
she doesn't give a damn—

i mean,
who could blame them?

—*her survival is quite the sight to behold, after all.*

most days,
she's a sweatpants girl;

on other days,
she's dressed to kill.

she sees the power in both—

she can revel in
her subtle beauty

just the same as
her accentuated beauty.

—*comfort & glamour.*

her exes?

they barely even cross her mind.

she doesn't hate them anymore, but she doesn't exactly think of them fondly either.

—*she simply feels nothing, & that's a win in her book.*

she went on to build
the most magical life in his wake,

& now he's
the one left wondering,

*what would it have been like
for me to be the one beside her now?*

—heaven for him | hell for her.

there was a time when she was convinced she wouldn't make it to her nineteenth birthday.

by some miracle, she did.

she's still alive.

& in a few months, she'll be thirty-two.

she doesn't often find herself wanting to die anymore, but that's not to say every day is easy.

on those really bad days, she thinks to herself, *at least i still have my horoscopes, my hazelnut lattes, & a familiar hand to hold.*

—*that's enough for her.*

they're both scorpios—

both moody as hell.
both a little distrustful.
both stuck in their own ways.

but they make it work.

—*no one could possibly get the other like they do.*

she's not a perfect partner—

she's a terrible cook
& an even worse baker,

she hates to drive
& she's on her phone too much,

she doesn't wash
her hair nearly enough,

she worries about things
that aren't that big of a deal,

& she has a habit of making
every conversation about herself.

—what's important is that she feels comfortable
enough not to be perfect around her.

her wife teaches her to brew her coffee

the long way,
the slow way.

she teaches her to live that way too—

forever reminding her
when she's doing too much

& not savoring her life nearly enough.

—*they never stop learning from each other.*

(homage to "i make my morning coffee the long way"
by parker lee.)

she doesn't post every photo

because

not everyone needs to know
everything that's going on in her life.

she doesn't post every poem

because

not everyone gets to know
how she's feeling or thinking.

—*she likes keeping some things for herself.*

she's a cancer—
rising

to the occasion
of feeling her feelings,

of finally letting
her heart have a voice.

—it hasn't always been easy for her.

she makes her own success.

there may be those who
have helped her along the way,

but they don't get to take all of the credit.

—*she doesn't think that makes her ungrateful.*

men everywhere
hate to see her thriving.

they seethe.
they throw tantrums.

they try (& fail) to
sabotage her again & again.

they can't stand seeing
a woman win in ways
they will never be able to.

—*that's how she knows she's made it.*

they told her,

"anyone can do what you do,"

to which she replied,

"okay, i'll wait."

—*she has a feeling she'll be waiting forever & ever.*

they pray for her downfall.

she prays that they
achieve everything they've ever wanted.

—*that's what she likes to call* class.

yes, she can see that
you're talking shit about her.

she's not ignoring you, exactly;

she's just saving her energy
for something that actually matters.

—*try not to be too sad about it.*

she isn't interested in being pit against
other successful women—

she knows that no one
could ever be as amazing as she is,

& she also knows that she
could never be as amazing as they are.

*—no two galaxies are the same, & there's so much
beauty in that.*

is she *cringe,*

or is she just embracing
her authentic self—

even the feminine parts society
convinced her to hate—

& that makes you
uncomfortable as hell?

—oh look, another excuse to spew hatred at women.

she's well aware
that people don't like her—

despise her, even.

she lets them say
whatever they want about her—

tear her down,

make a mockery of her
& her trauma—

it doesn't hurt anymore.

she's secure in who she is
& the value she brings to the world.

—doesn't seem like they are, though.

when she cried,
they cried the same tears.

when she screamed,
they screamed the same words.

when she empowered them,
they empowered her right back.

when she took steps to heal,
they were inspired to heal too.

*—she was never as alone as she thought | an author
& her readers.*

every time she thinks
she's fallen out of love with it,

it calls her all night, leaving
dozens of desperate voicemails.

it texts her seventy, eighty,
ninety, one hundred times.

it bangs on her door,
crying & begging to be let inside.

it throws rocks at her window,
shattering the panes.

even after all the damage it's caused,
she gives in every time.

—*poetry | the ex that never really stays an ex.*

sometimes her dreams & goals shift.

sometimes they morph into something totally unrecognizable.

it used to make her feel guilty, like she was letting down an old version of herself by going off & chasing something else.

but you know what?

as long as she's doing what she loves, she lights up from within, & in turn, she lights up the entire world around her.

—*look how brightly she glows.*

they told her
to follow the rules—

they told her
to follow the status quo—

they told her
to follow the established path—

& she proceeded to
give them the middle finger
& do everything
they told her she shouldn't.

—*because fuck that.*

she makes the brave decision—

even if it scares the shit out of her.
even if she knows she'll probably fail.

—at least it'll help her grow, right?

she's building herself an empire—

no, not for
the money or recognition

but because

she wants to know
that she lived & died doing

whatever the fuck makes her happy.

—*she'll figure the rest out.*

wanna know a secret?

once she stopped pretending
to be someone else
just to be liked by others,

she was finally free.

—*now she knows how important it is to like herself.*

these days, she meditates more. she drinks way too many cups of chamomile tea. she makes time for the little things that make her heart radiate with joy. she finally sees that there's so much more to life than always being productive or working, than always coming out on top.

—*it's about actually living.*

she smells like lavender,
rosemary, & a hint of starlight;

things happen to her that
shouldn't be possible;

she smiles as if she knows
things others don't;

& people seem to be
fascinated by her
or terrified of her.

—*she doesn't mind either way.*

don't be concerned if
she doesn't answer your text.

take it as a sign that
her skin is moisturized,
her candles are lit,
& her crystals are out.

she's probably busy
pulling tarot cards
or self-reflecting in
her journal.

with that said, she asks that you
please *don't* text her a second time.

—*her usual friday night.*

she still doesn't believe in god.

she certainly believes in her goddesses, though.

when she's done worshipping them, they give her a gentle yet fierce reminder to get on her knees & worship herself too.

—*she must say that no god has ever made her feel this empowered.*

go ahead—

jinx her.
hex her.
curse her.

spread lies like facts.

speak her name
with hate instead of love.

do your absolute worst.

she's more protected
than you know.

—*she's not worried.*

she is maiden—

there is a part of her that will
always be just slightly naive,
a part of her that sees
this world as a magical place
filled with possibility.

she is mother—

there is a part of her that will
always desire to create something,
a part of her that wants to
leave this place more beautiful
than it was before
she came into it.

she is crone—

there is a part of her that will
always think wistfully of the past,
a part of her that wonders
what it would have been like if
she had made different choices,
but she doesn't cling too tightly—
she views her regrets as lessons

& lets them go.

—*she's something of a triple goddess.*

you may think she's
all softness—all love, all light,

but, oh, how she
revels in her delicious shadows too.

—*she's full of surprises.*

sometimes she's so scared
to stand up for herself that

she thinks she must have been
a very powerful witch in a past life—

so powerful that it
scared the people around her

& she had no choice
but to hide, to be silent,

which is why she's vowed
to spend her current life

making it up to herself
by making her voice heard.

—there's more where that came from.

she's a believer in the idea that
rejection is redirection,

but she doesn't stop there—

she takes that rejection,
grinds it up with mortar & pestle,
& makes shimmering gold dust out of it.

—*transmutation spell.*

when she tells her friends
blessed be, what she means is:

> *i hope someone sends you*
> *a bouquet of your favorite flowers.*
>
> *i hope you find the perfect outfit,*
> *& you have just enough money for it.*
>
> *i hope you get to wake up*
> *& do what you love tomorrow*
> *& every single day after.*
>
> *i hope a stranger*
> *returns your kindness.*
>
> *i hope more good things*
> *happen to you, just because.*

when she tells her enemy
blessed be, it means the same thing.

—*sugar-laced words always taste sweeter.*

a dish of forever-tangled
jewelry—

a never-lit
lavender candle—

a finger-printed
amethyst crystal point—

a rarely used
bell to cast negativity away—

a too-tight
hairclip for her messy hair—

a sun-bleached oracle card
to remind her that
the world needs her ~~to get out of bed~~.

—on her nightstand.

finding her first sprout of white hair
wasn't nearly as devastating
as everyone told her it would be.

after all,

this is what it looks like to
have lived, to have loved,
to have hated, to have fought,
to have persisted as a woman does.

—*she welcomes more to grow in her midnight garden.*

the forest
is her church.

the sea
is her salvation.

neither

have ever tried
to convince her that

she's inherently incomplete
or sinful or lesser-than.

—*wholly.*

she's never felt compelled
to live her life by anyone else's book,

so she takes out her rose gold pen
& writes her own damn book,

& she's not afraid to go back
& cross shit out when it
no longer makes sense.

—*she finally found divinity in herself.*

she used to be afraid to sleep.

her dreams were filled with terrifying visions of the future that almost always came true—being betrayed by the people closest to her, mourning the deaths of those she loved so dearly.

she wished on every star she saw for the visions to be taken away, & so they were.

she didn't dream a single dream for years.

then one day it dawned on her: they hadn't meant to scare her. they had meant to *prepare* her.

she begged & pleaded for them to come back, but nothing seemed to change. after waiting for what seemed like an eternity, they eventually came trickling in—ever so cautiously at first, uncertain if she could handle them this time.

she could.

—*she can handle anything now.*

she wakes
by the sunlight

     & sleeps
     by the moonlight.

she rests
during wintertime

     & blooms
     during springtime.

she keeps
her loved ones close,

     & she lets them go
     if that's what they need.

—*she doesn't fight the cycles anymore.*

after all of the agony it caused her,
she used to be petrified of death,

but she's not anymore.

how could she be when
she knows it won't be the end?

she can come back as a wildflower,
or the butterfly that drinks its nectar,
or the book that presses its petals.

don't mistake this as a call for help;

she doesn't wish for death,
but she accepts whatever comes next.

—*her surrender.*

no, she will not be silent
about what happened to her—

the abuse, the neglect,
or the lifelong trauma.

she's proud to be breaking
all of these generational curses.

*—if you don't like it, then you can slip out through
the back door.*

she has a
much better relationship

with her mom
now that she's dead—

she talks to her every day,
offers her a cup of coffee,

looks for her *thank you*
in the form of break-in ladybugs.

some call her *peculiar.*
some call her *spiritual.*

—*perhaps she's a little bit of both.*

she's dangerous because

there's nothing anyone
could ever take away from her
that would make her feel inadequate,

because she would still have herself.

—*goddess help anyone who wishes to test her.*

people only seem to want one thing for a woman like her: to become a mother.

she knows that if she were to be one, she would be a much better one than the one she had, but she also knows that she would never be happy being one, & she chooses happiness every chance she gets.

good for her.

—*there's nothing selfish about that, ~~sorry~~.*

after her fever broke,
she looked around to see a society

somehow even more
broken than it was before—

stuck in a never-ending cycle
of false headlines, fearmongering, &

fine, who will we hate next?

when she looks around,
what she wants so desperately to see is

a society where
nobody ever has to be afraid

of existing as their
true & unrestricted selves.

—she won't stop holding on to hope.

she's learned not to have heroes—
aside from herself, of course.

*—too many of them turn out to be worse than any
villain on the page or screen.*

she considers herself a strong
& empowered woman,

& a strong & empowered woman
realizes that

another woman's experience
doesn't eclipse hers

or otherwise
take anything away from her.

—*when she says she champions women, she means*
all *women.*

whenever the world hurts,
she hurts too.

she's not naive—

she knows she's just
a tiny teardrop compared to

the whole ocean.

she knows that she's not big enough
to make all the changes we need,

but she wishes she was.

—aquarius moon.

for her, healing means
telling people who she really is,

even if she knows that
they won't understand or accept her.

—*good thing their approval isn't as important as her own.*

she will not be ashamed of
who she loves

or how she loves,

nor will she be ashamed
if those things change
as she changes.

—april 26, 2023 | an orange, white, & pink sunset.

nothing she does is for
a man's pleasure or attention.

some people's whole worldview
completely falls apart
when they find this out—

they can't even conceive of
a woman who exists for
anything else, let alone herself.

"then don't conceive of me,"
she says, laughing.

—*what an easy solution.*

her queerness is beautiful.

her queerness
is as soft as wild roses.

her queerness
is as strong as briar & thorn.

her queerness
is worthy of being respected.

her queerness
is worthy of being celebrated.

her queerness just *is*.

—*she is her queerness | her queerness is her.*

she is also *they.*

they're proud to be living their truth,
ignoring the hatred others throw their way.

—*bliss.*

people may say she's *different* now,
but all that reveals to her is
that they never really knew her
in the first place.

—*blindfolds off.*

when they dream about
the next cycle of their life,

they don't try to imagine
the exact details
of their transformation.

what they *do* try to imagine is
clarity & contentment

no matter who they may be.

—*complete & total acceptance.*

she might seem like
she has a plan for everything—

she might seem like
she has everything together—

when, in reality, she doesn't know
what the fuck she's doing most days.

—*& isn't that half the fun of existence?*

it was under a waxing moon
that the woman had been born.

they used to wish that
they could be full & bright,

but then they realized that
the moon is *always* whole—

it's all about
how you angle the light.

—*celestial are they.*

"one day, you aren't going to be
so worried about the things
you are right now.

though it may be hard to see,

everything will eventually
work out for the best.

though you may feel utterly lost,

you must remember that
you have never been so lost
that you couldn't find yourself again."

—*signed, your future self.*

acknowledgments

i. *my poet-wife, parker lee*—thank you for all of the booskerdoo runs that kept me sane & ultimately made this collection possible. <3

ii. *my literary agent, lauren spieller*—thank you for always being in my corner & helping me make dream after dream come true. you deserve an award.

iii. *my beta readers, summer webb & christine day*— thank you for always handling my work with care & tenderness, & also for finding all the mistakes i somehow missed the first hundred reads.

iv. *my illustrator, vylirium*—thank you for such breathtaking illustrations. it's been an absolute dream come true working with you.

v. *my friends & family*—thank you for your endless support & cheerleading. this is my tenth collection, so you have to be getting tired by now!

vi. *my readers*—thank you for your love & patience while i found my way to writing this.

about the author

amanda lovelace (she/they) is the author of several bestselling poetry titles, including her celebrated women are some kind of magic series as well as her you are your own fairy tale trilogy. they also write nonfiction books about witchcraft & cocreate tarot & oracle decks. when she isn't reading, writing, or drinking a much-needed cup of coffee, you can find her casting spells from her home in a (very) small town on the jersey shore, where she resides with her poet-wife & their three cats.

index

follow the author

@ladybookmad

@ladybookmad

@ladybookmad

amandalovelace.com

Andrews McMeel Publishing
a division of Andrews McMeel Universal
1130 Walnut Street, Kansas City, Missouri 64106

www.andrewsmcmeel.com

Illustrations by Vylirium

24 25 26 27 28 SDB 10 9 8 7 6 5 4 3 2 1

ISBN: 978-1-5248-9003-2

Library of Congress Control Number: 2024936605

Editor: Patty Rice
Art Director/Designer: Julie Barnes
Production Editor: David Shaw
Production Manager: Julie Skalla

ATTENTION: SCHOOLS AND BUSINESSES
Andrews McMeel books are available at quantity discounts
with bulk purchase for educational, business, or sales promotional use.
For information, please e-mail the Andrews McMeel Publishing
Special Sales Department: sales@amuniversal.com.